NBA MEGASTARS '99

D1290068

By Bruce Weber

SCHOLASTIC INC.

New York   Toronto   London   Auckland   Sydney
Mexico City   New Delhi   Hong Kong

Photo Credits
Cover/Poster/Back Cover (Duncan): NBA/Patrick Murphy-Racey. **Cover (O'Neil), 22, 23:** NBA/Andrew D. Bernstein. **Cover (Hardaway), 4, 10, 11, Back Cover:** NBA/Jon Hayt. **Cover (Garnett), 1, 9, 12, 27:** NBA/Nathaniel S. Butler. **Cover (Malone), 2, 18, 19, 20, 25:** NBA/Sam Forencich. **3 (Jordan), 5:** NBA/Fernando Medina. **3 (Duncan), 7:** NBA/D. Clarke Evans. **3 (Garnett), 8:** NBA/Dave Sherman. **3 (Van Horn), 29:** NBA/Louis Capozzola. **6, 26:** NBA/Glenn James. **13, 14, 15, 16, 30:** NBA/Scott Cunningham. **17:** NBA/Layne Murdoch. **21, 28:** NBA/Jerry Wachter. **24:** NBA/Jeff Reinking. **31:** NBA/Noren Trotman. **32:** NBA/Gary Dineen.

ISBN 0-590-05468-6

© 1999 by NBA Properties, Inc.
All rights reserved. Published by Scholastic Inc.

12 11 10 9 8 7 6 5 4 3 2 1   9/9 0 1 2 3 4/0

Printed in the U.S.A.
First Scholastic printing, February 1999
Book design: Michael Malone

The New Guard Takes Over

tim duncan

Everyone—even crazed Utah Jazz fans—went wild when **Michael Jordan** sank that 20-footer with 5.2 seconds to go last June. It was the perfect cap to the perfect season. MJ's endgame heroics precisely defined a **megastar**.

But as one season blends into the next, we've got to look at the coming megastars. That's why this latest edition highlights the old and the new. Sure, there's **The Mailman** and Michael and some surefire vets like **Tim Hardaway** and **Shawn Kemp**. But we're welcoming in some of the youngsters, too. That's why **Tim Duncan** and **Antoine Walker**, **Keith Van Horn** and **Kevin Garnett** are here right alongside the current masters.

Bottom line: The future is **brilliant**. America's pros, with help from the rest of the world's best—can you say **Zydrunas Ilgauskas**?—continue to dominate the world basketball scene. Today's athletes are **better, BIGGER, faster** and **stronger**, which makes every NBA game a war on the floor.

So sit back and enjoy. By next June, when the NBA crowns its 53rd champion, you'll have gotten your share of **thrills** from all of these megastars—and their teammates, too!

keith van horn

kevin garnett

Ray Allen

Who's the only **megastar** who went one-on-one with both Michael Jordan and actor Denzel Washington last year?

He's Got Game.

◆ Scored a career-high 40 points against Minnesota on April 18, 1998, hitting six of 10 from three-point range
◆ A premier free-throw shooter, Ray's career mark from the charity stripe is a solid 85.5%
◆ Voted Big East Player of the Year in 1996, averaging 23.4 points, 6.5 rebounds and 3.3 assists per game for the University of Connecticut

Sure, it's Ray Allen, star of stage, screen and court. The 6-5, 205-pounder lifted his game and his profile to incredible heights in '98. First, he proved that he's ready for anything in the NBA by averaging 19.5 points (up from 13.4 in '97) to lead the Bucks in the Central Division. Then he surprised basketball fans and shocked film critics with his fine performance in Spike Lee's hoop flick, *He Got Game*. Even a Knick fan like Spike had to rave about Ray's acting ability. As good as it was, however, it was nothing compared to his on-court performance for Milwaukee. Of course, if it doesn't work out in Milwaukee, Hollywood will always have a place for Ray. Wonder if he can sing?

"My **main focus,** as much as I have the ball, is to **make a play** that leads to a **basket** or some **free throws.**"

—Ray Allen

FUN FACT

Ray is an all-around good guy. His Ray of Hope Foundation provides food and clothing for the needy.

CAREER STATS:

POS	YRS	G	FG%	FT%	REB/RPG	AST/APG	STL	BLK	PTS/PPG
G	2	164	.429	.855	731/4.5	566/3.5	186	22	2,704/16.5

Tim Duncan

◆ Led all NBA rookies in scoring, rebounding, blocked shots and field-goal percentage: 1998

◆ NBA All-Defensive Second Team: 1998

◆ First selection in the 1997 NBA Draft

Has there ever been an NBA player with a better last name than San Antonio's **Tim Duncan**?

The Swimmer

And it's going to stay that way until a guy named Reboundin or Shootin comes along.

The former Wake Forest star came blasting onto the scene last year like few rookies in NBA history. He was Rookie of the Month every month, joining only Ralph Sampson (1983–84) and teammate David Robinson (1989–90) in that exclusive category. Somehow, when the Schick NBA Rookie of the Year votes were counted, New Jersey's Keith Van Horn managed to get three. Duncan had the other 113 votes!

Why not? Tim had a rookie season that most veterans can only dream of. He led the league in double-doubles with 57 and led his team in scoring 34 times. Not bad for a youngster who discovered basketball relatively late in life. That's right, Tim was an aspiring Olympic swimmer in his native Virgin Islands until he was 13 years old!

"By the second half of the season, I'd lost most of my _jitters_ and eliminated most of the bugs in my game. _That's when I started_ improving."

—Tim Duncan

FUN FACT

He may be seven feet tall and a great swimmer, but Tim says he's afraid of heights and sharks!

CAREER STATS:

POS	YRS	G	FG%	FT%	REB/RPG	AST/APG	STL	BLK	PTS/PPG
F/C	1	82	.549	.662	977/11.9	224/2.7	55	206	1,731/21.1

Kevin
Garnett

- Two-time NBA All-Star
- Earned his first career triple-double with 18 points, 13 boards and 10 assists against Denver in January, 1998
- Grabbed 18 rebounds in the opening game of the playoffs vs. Seattle, 1998

The last time Minnesota was this **excited** about a big man, his name was George Mikan, the NBA's first true megastar.

G-Man

It was the early 1950s. The home team was called the Lakers, the president was Dwight D. Eisenhower and Michael Jordan hadn't been born.

Times have changed in Minny. The G-Man, also known as Kevin Garnett, is in the building, leading the T-Wolves to the NBA playoffs. A one-time South Carolina schoolboy who finished his high school career in Chicago, the 22-year-old has become a dominant force in only his third year in the league. In the 1997–98 season, Kevin ranked in the top 20 in rebounds, steals, blocks and minutes. His 45 double-doubles ranked fourth in the league. No doubt about it. Kevin has a magnificent future. And he's only going to get better. Scary!

"I've learned a lot. **Most important, you need to stay positive and do all of the little things well.** **Put them all together and you'll be doing big things.**"

—Kevin Garnett

FUN FACT

Kevin grew up as the only male in a household with his mom and two sisters. "I learned respect by watching my mom work her tail off to support us," says Kevin.

CAREER STATS:

POS	YRS	G	FG%	FT%	REB/RPG	AST/APG	STL	BLK	PTS/PPG
F	3	239	.494	.737	1,905/8.0	729/3.1	330	444	3,662/15.3

Tim Hardaway

There's something **magical** about Tim Hardaway.

The Easy Way

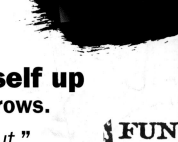

CAREER HIGHLIGHTS

◆ Tim scored a personal, playoff-high 38 points in Miami's Game 7 victory over the New York Knicks in the 1997 playoffs
◆ NBA All-Rookie First Team: 1989–90
◆ Five-time NBA All-Star

He knows exactly when he needs to take over a game. It's those Chicago playground smarts—and supreme confidence—he brings to the court. "It's a special instinct," says teammate Alonzo Mourning. "We need a big shot and you know Tim is going to take it."

"I'm used to the pressure and the physical play," says Hardaway. "That's the way I grew up on the playground. They'd bang you, kick you, stomp you, and then you'd bury the big shot."

Tim arrived in Miami from Golden State in 1996. At the end of the season, he was a free agent. Though he was rumored to be headed out of town, Tim hung with the Heat. Coach Pat Riley is delighted. "I may be biased," he says, "but I think Tim is the best point guard in the game."

"They may *knock* you down, but you've just got to pick yourself up and make a couple of free throws.

That's what this game is all about."
—Tim Hardaway

FUN FACT

In the 1997–98 season, when Hardaway had fewer than five assists, Miami went 3–7. When he had 10 or more, the Heat was 25–9.

CAREER STATS:

POS	YRS	G	FG%	FT%	REB/RPG	AST/APG	STL	BLK	PTS/PPG
G	8	612	.445	.777	2,210/3.6	5,573/9.1	1,166	103	11,991/19.6

Grant Hill

Forget Sara Lee.
Unless we missed someone, nobody doesn't like Grant Hill.

King of the Hill

And what's not to like? When he arrived in Detroit in 1994, he was already carrying big-time labels. Detroit fans called him "The Savior." NBA writers instantly dubbed him "The Next Michael." That would be enough to foul up most young men. But Grant took everything in stride, as he always does. Hill got his poise lessons early. His dad, Calvin, is one of the Dallas Cowboys' all-time greats; his mom, Janet, roomed with Hillary Clinton at Wellesley.

The next MJ? Grant is still the most likely candidate. A great all-around player who would probably rather hit a teammate for a basket than score one himself, he's second in the NBA's all-time list of triple-doubles. Only Michael has more—and Grant is only 26 years old!

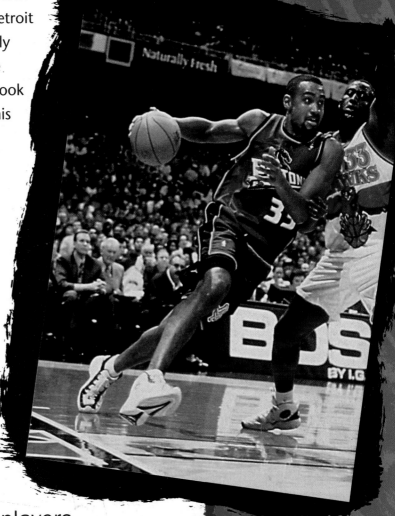

"It's not the coach or the other players.
It's me.
If I were playing better,
this wouldn't have happened."
— Grant Hill, after the Pistons got off to a slow start in the 1997–98 season

FUN FACT

When he's not on the court, working out or representing major American companies, Grant enjoys playing the piano. And, yes, he does that well, too!

CAREER STATS:

POS	YRS	G	FG%	FT%	REB/RPG	AST/APG	STL	BLK	PTS/PPG
F	4	311	.471	.734	2,572/8.3	2,035/6.5	511	211	6,434/20.7

Michael
Jordan

Michael Jordan will turn **50** on February 17, 2013.

Unforgetta-Bull

◆ Five-time NBA MVP:
1987–88, 1990–91, 1991–92,
1995–96, 1997–98
◆ Two-time Olympic gold
medalist: 1984, 1992
◆ Ten-time winner of NBA
scoring title
◆ Nine-time NBA All-Defensive
Team
◆ Led Bulls to six NBA titles:
1990–91, 1991–92, 1992–93,
1995–96, 1996–97, 1997–98

That's when he can begin play on the seniors golf tour. Until then, he should stay in the NBA. It's hard to imagine the day when he won't still be the greatest show on Earth.

If Michael's game has a weakness, no one has discovered it yet. Oh, Michael may have lost half a step. He doesn't drive into the middle of the jungle under the basket as often. And he might not be able to hang in the air forever anymore. But MJ is smarter than ever. He knows just how to use the great skills he still owns. With a game or a championship on the line, is there any other player in the universe you'd rather give the ball?

"**I know some** young players **try to imitate my** dunks. **But they were rarely planned.**

Once I got up in the air, I created them instinctively."

—Michael Jordan

FUN FACT

Years ago, MJ endorsed a line of Michael Jordan hair-care potions for Johnson Products. He stopped doing it—when he shaved his head!

CAREER STATS:

POS	YRS	G	FG%	FT%	REB/RPG	AST/APG	STL	BLK	PTS/PPG
G	13	930	.505	.838	5,836/6.3	5,012/5.4	2,306	828	29,277/31.5

Shawn
Kemp

- ◆ Six-time NBA All-Star
- ◆ Became first-ever Cavalier to start an All-Star game: 1998
- ◆ Starred for the Dream Team II, gold medal winners of the 1994 World Championship of Basketball
- ◆ Averaged 23.3 points and 10 boards per game during Seattle's NBA Finals battle with Chicago: 1996

Where else would a 29-year-old be called "**the old man**"?

Leading the Way

Nowhere but in Cleveland, where Shawn Kemp was one of only two non-rookies in the starting lineup most of last season. The Cavs traded for the powerful 6-10, 256-pounder before the 1997–98 season, with the NBA playoffs in mind. The pressure of being "the man" lifted Kemp's game to an all-time high.

Moving from the Seattle SuperSonics to the Cavs presented a real challenge to Kemp, who went from Concord (IN) High School to the pros in 1989—without playing a single game of college ball. "The big guys in the Eastern Conference are much more physical," says Kemp, who knows a thing or three about physical play. "They like to play in the paint, post up most of the time, and battle for every rebound." By leading the Cavs into the playoffs on the season's final day, you know that the "old warrior" adjusted just fine.

"In this league, you can't *pretend* what you're going to be.

I'm a pretty good **basketball player** and I **work hard**."

—Shawn Kemp

FUN FACT

Shawn dresses as "Santa Kemp" every Christmas to hand out toys to youngsters at local children's shelters.

CAREER STATS:

POS	YRS	G	FG%	FT%	REB/RPG	AST/APG	STL	BLK	PTS/PPG
F	9	705	.510	.730	6,723/9.5	1,293/1.8	883	1,049	11,590/16.4

Jason
Kidd

- One-time NBA All-Star (Jason was the first Dallas player to start an All-Star Game): 1996
- Schick NBA Co-Rookie of the Year (with Grant Hill): 1994–95
- Second overall pick of the 1994 NBA Draft
- Twice totaled more than 700 assists and 500 rebounds in a season, a feat accomplished by only Oscar Robertson, Magic Johnson, Wilt Chamberlain, Norm Van Lier and Micheal Ray Richardson

Did any player ever have a **rougher start** with a new team than Jason Kidd?

Back on Track

The second overall pick in the 1994 NBA Draft by Dallas, the ex-Cal All-American got off to a stupendous start with the Mavs. He shared Schick NBA Co-Rookie of the Year with Grant Hill in 1994–95. That's pretty good company. Jason was an NBA All-Star in his second season. But the following year, Jason was shipped to Phoenix in a trade that shocked most NBA fans. To make things even worse, Jason fractured his collarbone in his *first* game with the Suns. Since recovering, Kidd has been absolutely smashing. He runs the offense like an extra coach on the court, always among the NBA leaders in steals and assists. Plus, he can score when the situation calls for it. For the Phoenix Suns, the future suddenly looks very bright.

"I'm **happy** to be with the Suns. I hope I'm here for the next **ten years**. They're accustomed to **winning** and that's *exactly* where I want to be— with a **winner!**"

—Jason Kidd

FUN FACT

Jason collects baseball souvenirs. In fact, his number-one prize is an autographed bat from another kid, Seattle's Ken Griffey, Jr.

CAREER STATS:

POS	YRS	G	FG%	FT%	REB/RPG	AST/APG	STL	BLK	PTS/PPG
G	4	297	.394	.714	1,742/5.9	2,631/8.9	612	96	3,823/12.9

Karl
Malone

- ◆ NBA MVP: 1996–97
- ◆ Eleven-time NBA All-Star
- ◆ Two-time All-Star Game MVP: 1989, 1993 (Karl shared the award with teammate John Stockton)
- ◆ Named one of the 50 Greatest Players in NBA History

At the post office, every mail carrier knows the mail must get through **no matter what**.

Still Delivering

At the Delta Center in Salt Lake City, there's only one Mailman. He gets the job done every night, too.

When the Jazz picked Karl Malone in the first round of the 1985 NBA Draft, they took a gamble. Karl had been a good, not a great, college player. But he is the perfect example of what hard work can produce. With less than 4% body fat, Karl owns the NBA's most admired physique. The Mailman is a fearsome presence at both ends of the court.

Once a limited shooter, Karl is now deadly from as far as 18 feet out. He hits about 75% from the line, a huge improvement over the 48% mark he had his rookie year. In rain, sleet or snow, the Mailman continues to deliver big-time for the Jazz.

"Without a doubt, *I'm disappointed.* We fought **hard**, the guys did a good job. It's so *tough*, a tough loss for us."

—Karl Malone, following the Jazz's second straight loss in the NBA Finals

FUN FACT

Karl's wife, Kay, is a former Miss Idaho. And the two K's (Karl and Kay) have given birth to three more: daughters Kadee and Kaylee and son Karl, Jr.

CAREER STATS:

POS	YRS	G	FG%	FT%	REB/RPG	AST/APG	STL	BLK	PTS/PPG
F	13	1,061	.528	.727	11,376/10.7	3,499/3.3	1,513	874	27,782/26.2

Shaquille O'Neal

◆ **Six-time NBA All-Star**
◆ **First overall pick in the 1992 NBA Draft**
◆ **Schick NBA Rookie of the Year: 1992–93**
◆ **Led league in scoring: 1994–95 (29.3 ppg)**
◆ **Selected as one of the 50 Greatest Players in NBA History**

In Los Angeles—and the rest of the NBA—Shaquille O'Neal is, simply, **The Man**.

L.A.'s Main Man

At 7-1 and 315 pounds, Shaq is one of the largest humans on the planet. When he makes up his mind to go to the hole, look out. Because there isn't much anyone can do to stop him.

What separates O'Neal from the other big guys? It's his super athletic ability to go with his enormous size. Shaq runs the floor, passes well and often "out-quicks" opposing centers. And he's the biggest thing around without four wheels. When Shaq powers down the lane with the ball, well, anybody in the way is risking his health.

Sure, the Lakers are a talented bunch. Four of them made the West Squad at the 1998 All-Star Game. But it's the man in the middle who frightens opponents the most.

"If I have a bad game, I figure it's just one of those nights. The key for me is never having two bad games in a row."
—Shaquille O'Neal

FUN FACT

Shaquille O'Neal plans to become the author of a children's book in 1999.

CAREER STATS:

POS	YRS	G	FG%	FT%	REB/RPG	AST/APG	STL	BLK	PTS/PPG
C	6	406	.578	.535	5,012/12.3	1,017/2.5	328	1,115	11,054/27.2

Gary Payton

- ◆ **Second overall pick in the 1990 NBA Draft**
- ◆ **NBA Defensive Player of the Year: 1995–96**
- ◆ **Five-time NBA All-Star**
- ◆ **Olympic gold medalist: 1996**

If it's your responsibility to handle the ball against the SuperSonics, Gary Payton is your **worst nightmare**.

The Glove

The 1995–96 NBA Defensive Player of the Year, Gary has been a member of the All-Defensive First Team for five straight seasons. The Oakland, CA, native is a bundle of energy on the court. Wherever you look, he's there—going for a steal, deflecting a pass, disrupting opponents at every turn.

Gary is the guy who makes Seattle hop. On offense, his playmaking, penetration and shooting can dominate. And his defense can turn an opponent's game to mush. Gary is known as "The Glove" because he fits his man like one—no room to spare, no air to get off an easy shot.

Named *Sports Illustrated* College Player of the Year in 1990, Gary arrived in his first NBA camp as the Sonics' starting point guard and hasn't looked back since.

"I'm **excited** about our club in Seattle. We've got **great talent** and *great chemistry*. We're going to **win**."

—Gary Payton

FUN FACT

Gary is dedicated to helping kids. Every one of his favorite charities—Big Brothers, March of Dimes, the homeless, and more—is involved with young people.

CAREER STATS:

POS	YRS	G	FG%	FT%	REB/RPG	AST/APG	STL	BLK	PTS/PPG
G	8	654	.481	.711	2,462/3.8	4,380/6.7	1,494	139	10,419/15.9

David
Robinson

- **NBA MVP: 1994–95**
- **First overall selection in the 1987 NBA Draft (but didn't play until 1989, because of his Navy service)**
- **Eight-time NBA All-Star**
- **Led league in scoring: 1993–94 (29.8 ppg)**
- **Three-time U.S. Olympian: 1988, 1992, 1996**

What hasn't David Robinson **accomplished**?

The Admiral

He hasn't won a Nobel Prize, though he's capable of talking shop with winners. He hasn't made a hit record, though he's an outstanding saxophone and keyboard player. And he hasn't won an NBA title. Still, despite last year's conference semifinal loss to Utah, Robinson and fellow twin tower Tim Duncan are capable of bringing a championship to the Alamodome.

A one-time Naval Academy All-American and officer, "Admiral" Robinson has always had the talent. Now he has nine years of experience behind him. That enables him to be among the league leaders in scoring, rebounds, field-goal percentage and blocks. And that's saying a lot. David has already been voted one of the 50 Greatest Players in NBA History. But personal accomplishments aside, the Admiral still wants that big ring.

"I'm focused on that championship. Lots of *pretty good* teams haven't made it. But our team has great potential. We need to reach for it."
—David Robinson

FUN FACT

If he weren't a basketball player, Robinson would like to have been a scientist or a musician.

CAREER STATS:

POS	YRS	G	FG%	FT%	REB/RPG	AST/APG	STL	BLK	PTS/PPG
C	9	636	.524	.745	7,389/11.6	1,925/3.0	1,004	2,204	15,940/25.1

Keith
Van Horn

◆ Scored 17 points and grabbed 10 rebounds in the Schick NBA Rookie Game at the 1998 All-Star Weekend

◆ Established his career high with 33 points against Toronto, April, 1998

◆ Keith was a three-time All WAC player in college, the only player in league history to accomplish the feat

The New Jersey Nets' Continental Airlines Arena sits on a spot that was formerly **swampland**.

No Doubt About It

Unfortunately, over the years, the Nets' play often matched the neighborhood. But the arrival of Keith Van Horn may have changed all that—for a long time to come.

After Keith missed the first 17 games of his rookie season with a sprained ankle, some fans were discouraged. But as they say in the Garden State, "Fuhgeddaboutit." The 6-10 Van Horn scored 11 points in his first game (a Nets win), followed with 30 a week later (another Nets win), and kept right on rolling. Though it took the team until the last game of the season to sew up a playoff berth, there was never a question about Keith Van Horn. Shooting, passing, rebounding—just *knowing* the game—Keith can flat-out play.

"I *believe* in a **strong work ethic**. That single **factor** can take your **game** a **long** way."

—Keith Van Horn

FUN FACT

Keith broke his toe at midseason last year and missed three games. With his work ethic, however, he continued to work on his game!

CAREER STATS:

POS	YRS	G	FG%	FT%	REB/RPG	AST/APG	STL	BLK	PTS/PPG
F	1	62	.426	.846	408/6.6	106/1.7	64	25	1,219/19.7

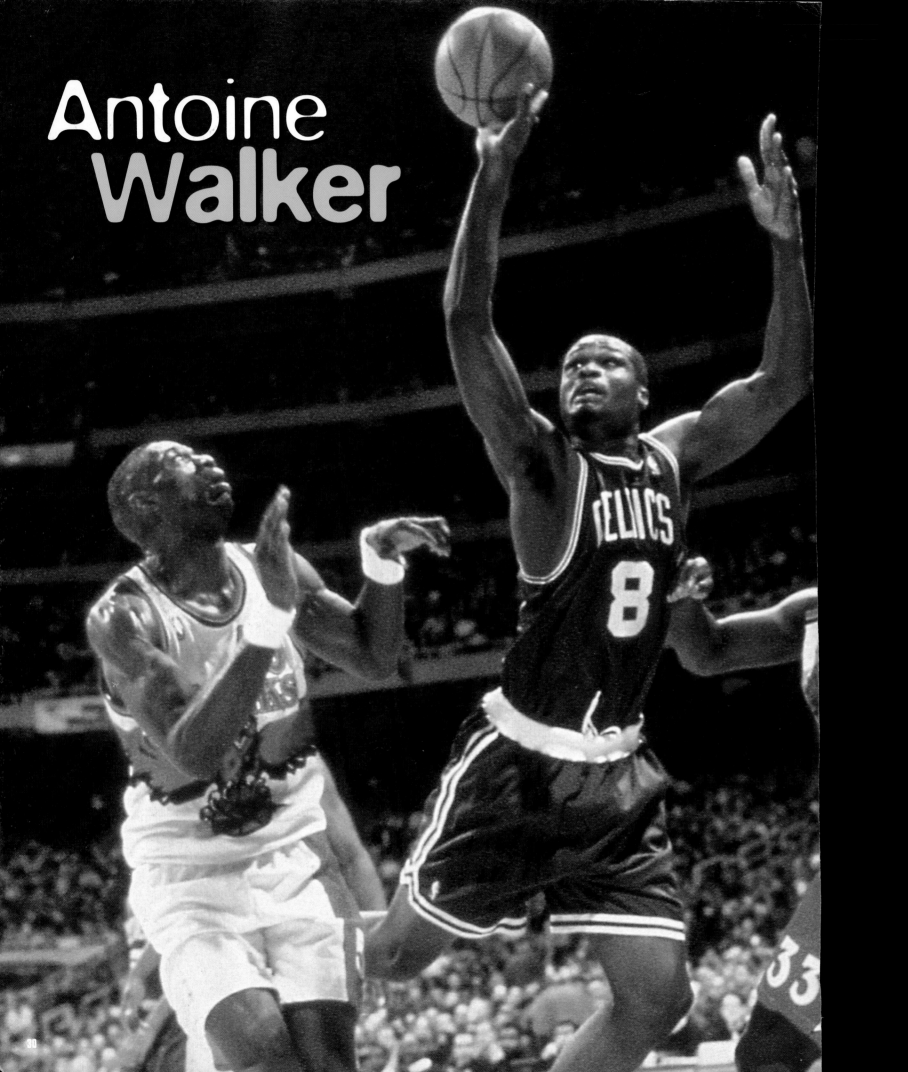

Antoine Walker

Don't look now but the **Boston Celtics** are on the way back.

The Kentucky Connection

◆ Only three Celtics (Larry Bird, Kevin McHale and Sam Jones) have ever scored more than the 49 points Antoine tallied against Washington in January, 1998
◆ As a rookie, he led the team in scoring (17.5), rebounds (9.0) and blocks (53)
◆ NBA All-Rookie First Team: 1996–97
◆ NBA All-Star: 1998

The biggest winners in NBA history, the Celts had fallen on hard times. But now, thanks to a couple of ex-Kentucky Wildcats, the glory days are coming again in Boston.

Everyone credits coach Rick Pitino, who once coached Kentucky to a national title. But the real hero is Antoine Walker, Pitino's star then and now. At 6-9 and 245, Walker features strength, speed and serious hops. "I'm not a classic power forward," says Walker. "My game is quickness, going around opponents to the basket." And is he ever quick. Playing in the same Pitino system for so many years has helped Walker adjust from college to the pros. After a great rookie season in 1996–97, Antoine made tremendous progress the following year, averaging 22.4 points and 10.2 rebounds per game.

"I'm still *adjusting* to playing **power forward**. I think I can *handle the ball* on the floor and in the **air** well enough. But I **know** I'm going to have to get **stronger**."

—Antoine Walker

FUN FACT

Walker's "Antoine's Crazy 8's" hosts 44 Boston area youngsters at every Celtic home game. Each guest gets a game ticket, transportation, a T-shirt and refreshments.

CAREER STATS:

POS	YRS	G	FG%	FT%	REB/RPG	AST/APG	STL	BLK	PTS/PPG
F	2	164	.424	.639	1,577/9.6	535/3.3	247	113	3,275/20.0

ODDS & ENDS

1998 ALL-NBA TEAM

F Karl Malone, *Utah*
F Tim Duncan, *San Antonio*
C Shaquille O'Neal, *Los Angeles*
G Michael Jordan, *Chicago*
G Gary Payton, *Seattle*

1998 ALL-DEFENSIVE TEAM

F Scottie Pippen, *Chicago*
F Karl Malone, *Utah*
C Dikembe Mutombo, *Atlanta*
G Michael Jordan, *Chicago*
G Gary Payton, *Seattle*

1998 ALL-ROOKIE TEAM

Tim Duncan, *San Antonio*
Keith Van Horn, *New Jersey*
Zydrunas Ilgauskas, *Cleveland*
Brevin Knight, *Cleveland*
Ron Mercer, *Boston*

1997–98 NBA AWARD WINNERS

NBA Most Valuable Player
Michael Jordan, *Chicago*

IBM Coach of the Year
Larry Bird, *Indiana*

Schick NBA Rookie of the Year
Tim Duncan, *San Antonio*

NBA Defensive Player of the Year
Dikembe Mutombo, *Atlanta*

NBA Sixth Man
Danny Manning, *Phoenix*

NBA Most Improved Player
Alan Henderson, *Atlanta*

ATLANTIC DIVISION

1. Miami Heat
2. New Jersey Nets
3. New York Knicks
4. Boston Celtics
5. Orlando Magic
6. Washington Wizards
7. Philadelphia 76ers

CENTRAL DIVISION

1. Indiana Pacers
2. Atlanta Hawks
3. Chicago Bulls
4. Detroit Pistons
5. Charlotte Hornets
6. Cleveland Cavaliers
7. Milwaukee Bucks
8. Toronto Raptors

MIDWEST DIVISION

1. San Antonio Spurs
2. Utah Jazz
3. Houston Rockets
4. Minnesota Timberwolves
5. Dallas Mavericks
6. Vancouver Grizzlies
7. Denver Nuggets

PACIFIC DIVISION

1. Los Angeles Lakers
2. Phoenix Suns
3. Seattle SuperSonics
4. Los Angeles Clippers
5. Sacramento Kings
6. Portland TrailBlazers
7. Golden State Warriors

EASTERN CONFERENCE CHAMPIONS
Indiana Pacers

WESTERN CONFERENCE CHAMPIONS
Los Angeles Lakers

NBA WORLD CHAMPIONS
Los Angeles Lakers